The
Animal Kingdom

ANIMAL EVOLUTION

Malcolm Penny

Illustrated by Jackie Harland

The Bookwright Press
New York · 1987

The Animal Kingdom

Animal Evolution
Animal Homes
Animal Migration
Animals and their Young

First published in the
United States in 1987 by
The Bookwright Press
387 Park Avenue South
New York, NY 10016

First published in 1987 by
Wayland (Publishers) Ltd
61 Western Road, Hove
East Sussex BN3 1JD, England

ISBN 0-531-18121-9
Library of Congress Catalog Card Number: 87-70388

Typeset by DP Press, Sevenoaks, Kent, England
Printed by Casterman S.A., Belgium

Contents

A detective story

A fossil of the prehistoric bird-reptile, archaeopteryx. Like a reptile, this creature had claws, teeth and a long, bony tail. Like a bird, however, it had feathers and could fly.

If you could travel back in time for hundreds of millions of years, what animals would you see on earth? You would find it hard to recognize any of them. There has been life on earth for over three billion years, and during that time living things have changed a great deal.

The way in which living things have changed is called evolution. Modern animals have evolved from ancient animals. They had to change because the world around them was changing. In this book we shall ask how evolution happened, but first, and perhaps more important, how do we know?

The truthful answer is that we can never be absolutely certain, but, like a detective studying the scene of a crime, we can find evidence that leads us to the most likely answers. For example, no human being ever saw a living dinosaur, and yet we know not only that they existed, but when they lived, how big they were, roughly what they looked like, and even what they ate. We know these things because of the evidence, and because of the work of some great scientific detectives.

The evidence for evolution comes partly from fossils, and from knowing the age of the rocks in which we find them. As we shall learn in this book, animals are still evolving now, and will continue to do so for as long as there is life on earth. This book is the detective story so far.

Opposite *A scene during the reign of the dinosaurs. Two brontosauruses graze in a lake, while a triceratops feeds at the water's edge. The carnivorous (flesh eating) tyrannosaurus rex stands in the foreground. Above them swoop prehistoric bird-reptiles called pterodactyls. The plants shown are prehistoric horsetails.*

The importance of fossils

The fossils shown here tell us how some creatures looked millions of years ago.

When an animal dies, the parts of it that are not eaten by scavengers usually rot away until there is nothing left. However, in certain conditions, especially under water, the hard parts of an animal will be preserved. Sand or silt settles over them, and over many centuries a chemical change takes place. The bone or shell is turned to stone, and the remains are said to be fossilized.

Layer upon layer of silt may fall, until the fossil is buried many feet deep. As the silt is tightly packed under the weight of the layers above, it turns to rock and the fossil is preserved for ever in the rock.

However, the fossil may not always stay hidden. Under the earth's surface there are great movements that can twist rocks and push them upward.

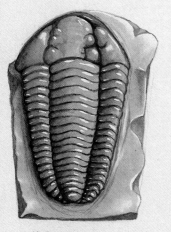

Trilobite
over 250 m years old

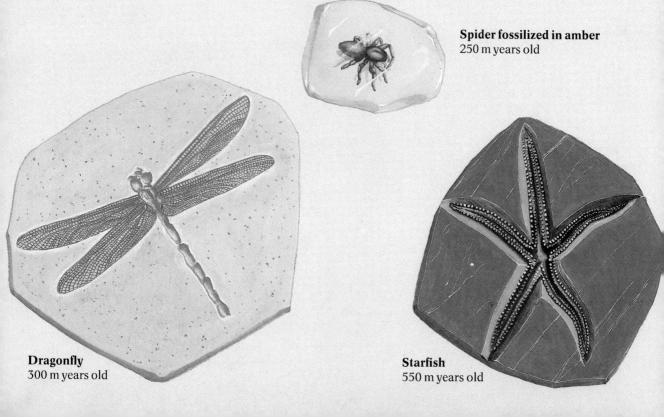

Spider fossilized in amber
250 m years old

Dragonfly
300 m years old

Starfish
550 m years old

Eventually, the rock with the fossil may become part of dry land. Sooner or later, the rock will be weathered away until the fossil is exposed to the air. One day, a scientist may find himself looking at it, perhaps a hundred million years after the fossilized animal died.

The age of rocks can be figured out by geologists, who can find out in which order the various layers of rock were laid down. The best place to see layers of rock is in a huge hole in the ground like the Grand Canyon. The oldest rocks (2 billion years old) are right at the bottom and the youngest ones at the top. The canyon contains many important fossils.

Scientists can also measure the tiny amount of radioactivity in the fossils themselves, which tells how old they are. By collecting fossils, and knowing the age of each one, we can begin to see how a type of animal has changed over millions of years.

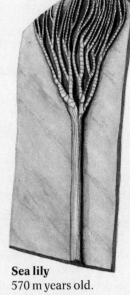

Sea lily
570 m years old.
Some creatures
very similar to
this sea lily
exist today.

Lariosaurus, a reptile
150 m years old

Ammonite
225 m years old

Disasters and evolution

Geologists have found fossil shells high above sea level, even on huge mountains like Mount Everest. This shows that most of the earth's surface has been covered by water at one time or another. Other parts, which were once dry land, have been flooded in mighty movements of the earth's crust. Many islands have been created in this way.

Changes in sea level have also been brought about by ice ages, when the water in the sea froze into the ice caps at the poles. When this happened, the sea level fell by hundreds of feet, only to rise again when the ice melted.

These changes in the earth's appearance took millions of years to happen, and they caused a series of disasters. Fish were stranded as their shallow seas dried up, and other animals were drowned as the waters rose again. Some of each were fossilized. The tops of some mountains became islands when the land was flooded, as the sea level rose higher.

The diagram below shows the position of the continents 200 million years ago (left) and today (right). The arrows indicate direction of movement.

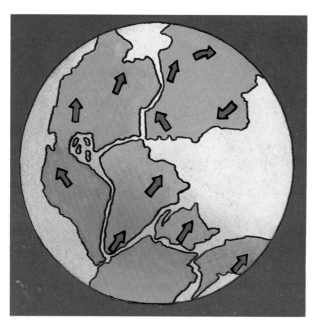 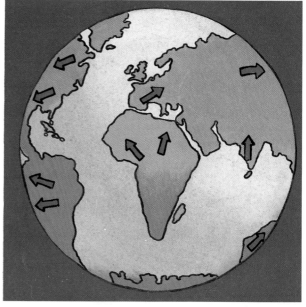

Groups of animals living on these cut-off islands have evolved differently from their relatives in other parts of the world.

Another cause of changes to animal life is called "continental drift." The continents are slowly moving all the time. They float on the red-hot, molten rocks beneath them, and tend to wander apart. Although Australia and South America are thousands of miles apart today, they once were both joined to Antarctica. We know this because fossils of the same species, and even the same species of living plants and animals, have been found in all three continents.

The extinction of the great dinosaurs may have been caused by a dramatic change in the earth's climate, making it impossible for them to survive.

The prehistoric-looking land iguana lives on the Galapagos islands. Many of the animals of these islands have evolved in isolation and so are not found anywhere else.

9

The timescale of evolution

From the fossil evidence available, scientists estimate that life on earth began about 3½ billion years ago. Over many millions of years microscopic living organisms began to develop, until about 500 million years ago primitive shellfish, jellyfish and worms appeared.

Within the next 200 million years, the process of evolution speeded up. During this period fish were the first to develop. Later, some fish evolved lungs to breathe and simple limbs, which meant that they could therefore venture onto the land. They became the first amphibians.

Next to appear were flying insects and the reptiles. Scientists have studied the skeletons of snakes that exist today. They have found tiny bones in the skeletons that suggest that snakes originally evolved from four-legged reptiles.

The bar chart shows the periods of time that different kinds of animals have lived on earth.

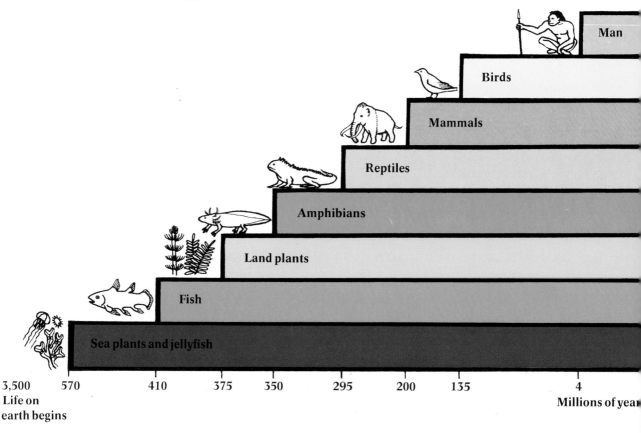

Man

Birds

Mammals

Reptiles

Amphibians

Land plants

Fish

Sea plants and jellyfish

3,500   570   410   375   350   295   200   135   4
Life on
earth begins   Millions of years

The tuatara, a lizard that lives on a few small islands in New Zealand. It is very similar to reptiles that lived 200 million years ago.

Between 230 and 60 million years ago, dinosaurs were alive. During this period some reptiles began to fly, birds evolved and early mammals appeared. After the dinosaurs died out 60 million years ago, mammals evolved rapidly. Some went from the land to the sea and became the ancestors of our whales and seals.

Over 30 million years ago the first apes appeared. Later some apes lived in open grasslands, and about 4 million years ago the first ape-men developed and became our ancestors.

It is hard to think in terms of hundreds of millions of years. Instead we could imagine that all life on earth evolved within 24 hours – one day, beginning at 12:00 a.m. If this were so, dinosaurs appeared at 11:00 p.m. and died out at 11:40 p.m. Human beings appeared at the last minute – at 11:59 p.m! So we are very young compared with the age of the earth.

Gradual changes

Why is it that some animal species have survived while others have died out? The answer is that to survive, an animal must change and adapt when necessary.

All animals of the same species, including humans, differ slightly from one another. People have different colored skin and eyes, they may be tall or short, and their hair may be dark or fair, straight or curly. On the other hand, people usually look more or less like their parents.

People had been breeding dogs and horses for centuries, by selecting which individuals to mate to provide the sort of animal they wanted, before anyone realized that the same thing goes on in nature. When it was discovered, the process was called "natural selection."

Dalmatian

Afghan hound

Dachshund

Natural selection works by allowing individuals to survive, and to produce young that resemble them, only if they are properly equipped to live in their environment. When the environment changes, the type of individual that can survive to breed will also change. If no member of a species can adapt to its environment, the species will become extinct.

The individuals that survive best, and leave the most offspring, are those with an advantage over the others. Think of eyes, for example. A successful eagle must have perfect eyesight, to be able to find food. Nocturnal animals like bushbabies have evolved huge, sensitive eyes, so they can see in the dark. Moles, however, do not need eyes, but have evolved especially strong feet for digging.

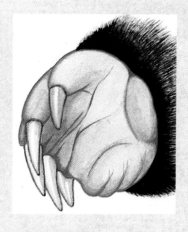

The mole's front paws are shaped like shovels and are well suited to digging.

Breeders have produced hundreds of varieties of dogs. The ones shown below differ from one another in size, shape and type of coat.

Old English sheepdog

English springer spaniel

Wire-haired foxterrier

Growing apart

The changes that make an animal successful in a particular way of life are called "adaptations." Some adaptations enable a species to survive a change in its environment. The ancestors of whales and seals, for example, adapted themselves so that they could live in the sea, instead of on the land. Other animals have adapted themselves to be able to run faster than their competitors, or to become more attractive to a mate, or to eat different food.

Suppose a species of animal lived by browsing, that is, by eating the leaves from bushes. As the species grew in numbers, there would be competition among animals to get to the bushes before the leaves were all eaten. Now imagine that some of the animals had slightly different mouths, which made it easier for them to graze, that is, to eat grass. They would not need to take part in the competition for the bushes, but they would still be well-fed and able to produce healthy young. The young would tend to have the same slightly different mouths as their parents.

Eventually, the two groups would become separate, but able to live together in the same area. One species would have split into two. Well, this actually happened millions of years ago in Africa, when the browsing black rhinoceros and the grazing white rhinoceros became different species – though it is not certain which came first.

If groups of animals of the same species live far apart, and never meet to breed, each group may evolve in a slightly different way. Many animals that live on islands have become separate species, even though they have close relatives on nearby islands. This is because they never cross the water to meet each other.

Opposite *The black rhino has evolved to browse on bushes, while the white rhino grazes on grass. The giraffe has evolved a long neck to reach high branches.*

14

Evolving to feed

The black and white rhinoceroses in Africa became adapted to eat different kinds of food in order to avoid competition. This is a common way for new species to appear.

At a bird table, different birds can feed in different ways without having to fight. Sparrows, robins and starlings feed on top of the table, while chickadees can eat from a hanging bag of suet. Elsewhere in the garden, blackbirds pounce on worms, while thrushes break snail shells to eat their contents.

Birds have very different shaped beaks depending on what they eat. A bird of prey needs a large, hooked beak, while a wader uses its very long bill for digging in the sand.

Every species of animal is adapted to eat a particular diet. Some of the adaptations are more obvious than others – think of a giraffe's neck.

A butterfly's long proboscis can reach deep inside flowers to find nectar. The anteater's long, sticky tongue easily picks up ants and termites. The parrot's strong beak is useful for cracking nuts.

Butterfly

Parrot

Anteater

16

Once, millions of years ago, giraffes had ordinary necks. However, there must have come a time when the competition from other browsing animals meant that only the tallest giraffes could feed, by being able to reach higher up in the bushes. The tall giraffes would tend to produce tall young. So they and their tall offspring would survive better than giraffes with shorter necks. Soon – which means in a few million years when we talk of evolution – long-necked giraffes were the only kind to be seen.

A long neck was an advantage in another way to the giraffe. Although they had become too tall to run fast to escape their enemies, they could see danger coming a long way off, and so would have sufficient time to escape.

The same type of story accounts for all adaptations for feeding, from the powerful front legs and sticky tongue of the aardvark (the African anteater) to the strong grinding teeth that enable the zebra to eat the toughest grass.

The elephant's trunk can pull off branches and feed leaves into the animal's mouth. The tortoise has no teeth. It cuts up leaves with its horny, sharp mouth parts. The tiger's sharp teeth are well adapted for eating raw flesh.

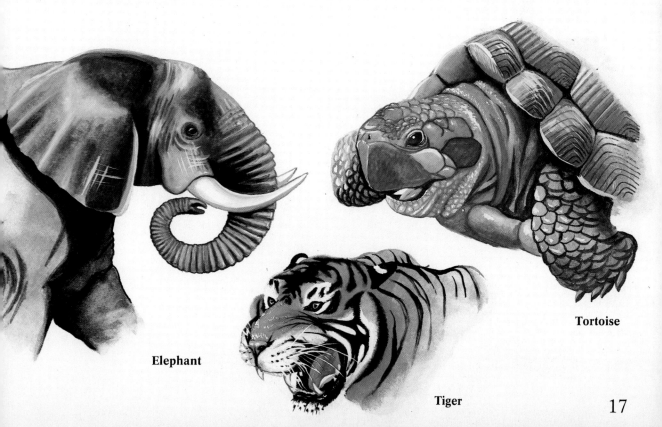

Elephant

Tortoise

Tiger

Fine feathers

Some animals have become adapted to attract and keep a mate during the breeding season. The most famous of these adaptations is the peacock's tail with its shimmering beautiful colors. The tail is only useful for displaying to a female. It is so large and heavy that it makes it difficult for the bird to fly.

There are other very spectacular male plumages like those of the birds of paradise and lyre-birds of New Guinea, which display their superb tail feathers to the females. Some Asian pheasants are brightly colored, as are the macaws, tanagers and quetzals of South America.

Male butterflies, too, are often more brightly colored than the females. Like the birds, they have evolved their bright colors by the process called "sexual selection." This means that females of such species breed more often with the most colorful males of the species.

However, the process also works the other way. The males of some species, like sparrows, are rather dull colored. The males have kept their dull appearance because the females did not breed with brightly colored individuals. The breeding colors of most animals enable them to recognize males and females of their own species.

This male butterfly, Urania croesus, *from Madagascar, is brightly colored to attract a female.*

If the males fight for the chance to breed, those that are large and powerful have the advantage. They win the fights and have the most offspring. Stags, and stag beetles which are named after them, antelope and buffalo all have horns whose main purpose is to fight other males in the breeding season. The victor will attract the females.

It need not always come to a fight – fighting is dangerous to both animals involved. The bright colors of tropical fish or the throat-pouches of some lizards are used in "displays," which will drive other males away before they come too close.

A male peacock displays his gorgeously colored tail to two peahens, which are less colorful.

Predators and prey

The evolution of some animals is affected by others. For example predators and their prey have affected one another. Often both must be fast runners with long legs. There are different kinds of legs. A hunting cat, such as a cheetah, has four toes on each foot, with sharp claws. The claws grip the ground and also grasp the animal's victim. An antelope has only two toes, with horny toenails, purely for running.

There are also differences between the eyes of a predator and those of a non-hunting animal. Both need sharp eyesight. The predator needs forward vision, for judging distances, while the prey needs all-around vision, to see the predator coming. A fox has its eyes at the front of its head, while a rabbit has them at the sides.

It helps both predator and prey if they are camouflaged, which means they are hard to see because of their colors. Many have stripes or spots, to blend with the dappled shadows in woodland. Those in the open African plains are colored to match the background. Lions blend in perfectly with the savannah, as do the gazelles they hunt.

The best camouflage is found among animals with many predators. For caterpillars, moths or small fish in the ocean, the only defense is to be nearly invisible. Many moths look like the bark of a tree, and fish may imitate seaweed, or hide among coral.

The camouflage of moths is useless to them at night when they fly. Their main enemies, bats, are nearly blind, but have evolved an acute sense of hearing. They hunt by sound, listening for the echoes of their own high-pitched squeaks, and they find moths easily, even in complete darkness.

The cheetah's strong paws are well adapted for running at high speed, while the slender hooves of the Thomson's gazelle enable it to run and leap.

Mammals in the ocean

One of the most extraordinary chapters in the story of evolution concerns the invasion of the sea by land animals. At least three separate groups of air-breathing, land mammals have become perfectly adapted to life in the ocean.

The first group are the seals and sea lions, whose ancestors were creatures somewhat like our modern bears. Some ancestors of our elephants became dugongs and manatees, the second group of sea mammals. Like elephants, they have trunks and feed on plants. Scientists believe that manatees evolved from elephants because the females produce milk for their young from exactly the same place as modern elephants do – from teats between their front legs.

You can see the similarity between an elephant and a manatee in this photograph. Like elephants, manatees feed on vegetation.

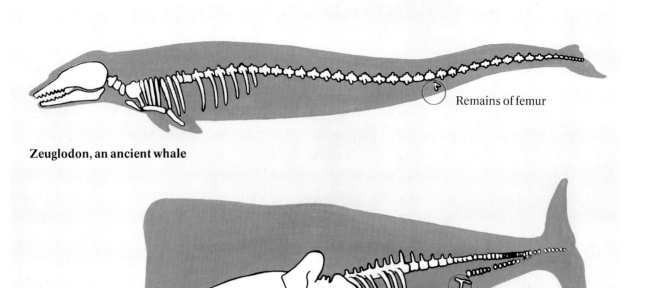

Zeuglodon, an ancient whale

Remains of femur

Remains of femur

Sperm whale

The last group is the whales. Fossils show that they are related to the family of land animals that includes pigs and hippopotamuses. Even today there are bones in a whale's body that suggest it once had hind legs. The front legs it once used for walking have become paddles for swimming.

Fifty million years ago, when early whales were alive, most of what is now Europe and the Mediterranean formed a large shallow sea. Whale-like fossils have been found where ancient rivers flowed into this sea.

Modern hippos live in rivers and eat plants, but evidence suggests that their ancestors ate meat as well. With an effort, we can imagine how some ancient hippos might have gone deeper into the river to chase fish, thus avoiding the competition for food in the muddy shallows. Gradually they adapted to ocean life and became the lovely streamlined giants we know as whales.

This diagram compares the skeletons of a prehistoric whale, zeuglodon, and a modern sperm whale. Circled in red is the bone that remains from the hind legs of the whale's land-dwelling ancestors.

Knowhow

We have looked at some ways in which animal bodies have been adapted over millions of years. But their behavior can also evolve. Animal behavior can be very complicated, like the mating dances of some insects, the courtship behavior of fish, or the nest-building of some birds. The animals do not have to learn how to do these things – they know from the moment they are born. Such behavior is called "instinctive behavior," and it has been developed after many thousands of generations of evolution.

It is easy to see that an insect that gets its courtship dance wrong will not attract a mate. And a bird that cannot build a good nest will not be able to rear its young. So neither of these clumsy creatures will have a chance to pass on its ignorance to the next generation.

Scorpions perform a complicated courtship dance before mating.

Instinctive behavior does have a serious drawback: it cannot be changed if something unexpected occurs. Jackdaws (European birds of the crow family) often make their nests by dropping twigs into a hole in a tree until the hole is nearly full. If one chooses the chimney of a house instead of a hole in a tree, it will drop twigs into it endlessly and never finish its nest. The jackdaw does not know the difference and cannot change its behavior.

There are some animals that have the ability to change their behavior by learning to cope with new situations. They may find a new kind of food, or learn to use a different nest-site, unlike the poor jackdaw. The ability to change behavior in such ways is called "intelligence." The evolution of intelligence was a great advance in the development of animal life.

A male satin bowerbird of eastern Australia has positioned stones, shells and flowers to decorate his bower.

Great brains

Some birds show signs of intelligence. In Britain, bluetits (relatives of our chickadees) learned to open milk bottle tops to reach the cream. Cats and dogs respond to their names and show other signs of intelligence. Dogs, in particular, can learn quite complicated actions. Some breeds can be trained to guide a blind person safely through busy streets.

The most intelligent animals are apes and monkeys, which belong to the primates. This word means "among the first," or "chief." They evolved their greater intelligence because of changes that took place in the shape of their hands and their brains.

The hands which evolved for swinging in the trees became useful for picking up stones and twigs. Chimpanzees use stones to crack nuts, or twigs to dig out termites from their nest to eat. They can also throw sticks at their enemies.

Swinging in the trees needs very good eyesight, as well as grasping hands. As their eyesight improved, the apes had less need for their sense of smell. They could look at things instead of sniffing them. Gradually the part of the brain that deals with the sense of smell became smaller, allowing more room in the skull for the "thinking part" of the brain to grow larger. In this way primates became more intelligent.

The orangutans of Borneo are very intelligent primates, having many skills and good memories. They know where to look for food in the forest at different times of year. Even more intelligent are the gorillas in Africa. In captivity some have been taught to "speak" to humans in sign language.

Humans, however, can understand much more complex language, and can read and write.

Opposite *Chimpanzees use their intelligence and learn to dig out ants from their nests and to crack nuts open with stones.*

Humans and evolution

Less than a hundred years ago, people found it very hard to believe that humans are primates, related to the great apes. Now the evidence is so strong that most people accept it.

Many fossils have been found, mostly skulls, jaws and teeth, mixed with stone tools. They show that a creature that walked upright and had a large brain lived in northern Kenya as long as four million years ago. While this creature had some ape-like feaures, such as a bony ridge above its eyes, and jaws that stuck out beyond its flat nose, scientists believe it was an ancestor of modern human beings.

How did this creature evolve? About five or six million years ago, the climate became drier. A new type of landscape appeared with large areas of open grassland between the forested areas.

Scientists who have studied evolution believe that humans evolved in the order shown below.

Australopithecus
over 3 m years old

Homo erectus
500,000 to 300,0
years old

Upright apes, which could move easily in the open country, could escape competition for food within the forests. These creatures gradually evolved into human beings and spread out across the whole world.

Humans are a very new kind of animal, considering how old the earth is. We still have left-overs from our earlier existence. As we have evolved, our appendix, our little toes, and the muscles to move our ears have lost their value to us.

As we have seen, animals evolve slowly and gradually as their world changes. In the past, such changes took many thousands of years to occur. Today humans can rapidly destroy forests and build cities, using powerful machinery. Sad to say, many animals do not have time to adapt to these changes and so are dying out. The good news is that we are the only animal that has evolved the wish to protect the other creatures, with which we share the world.

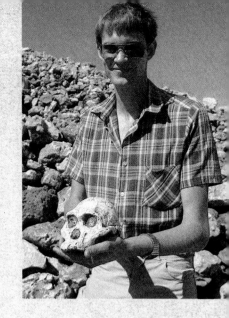

A scientist holds a woman's skull, discovered in South Africa. The skull is thought to be 3 million years old.

Neanderthal man
110,000 to 35,000 years old

Early Homo sapiens
35,000 years old

Glossary

Amphibian A cold blooded creature that lives on land, but breeds in water.

Ancestor A person (or creature) from whom another is directly descended.

Browsing Eating the leaves of trees and bushes.

Camouflage Coloring or shape that hides an animal by making it look like its natural surroundings.

Continental drift The theory that the earth's continents are slowly moving over the surface of the planet.

Diet The whole range of food that an animal eats.

Display Behavior that shows the mood of an animal to others, usually during mating or as a warning of a fight.

Environment The world around us, or our surroundings, which includes plants and animals, water and soil.

Evidence Findings that confirm a theory as true or false.

Extinct No longer in existence; having died out.

Fossil Hardened remains or prints of plants or animals that lived years ago.

Geologist A person who studies the rocks that form the earth.

Grazing Eating grass.

Instinctive behavior Behavior that does not have to be learned, sometimes called "in-born" behavior

Intelligence The ability to change behavior in response to new circumstances.

Mammal A warm-blooded animal whose females feed their young with milk.

Mate A breeding partner belonging to the opposite sex.

Molten Melted.

Natural selection The process that results in the greatest number of young being produced by the animals that are best adapted to their environment.

Predator An animal that lives by eating other animals, which are called prey.

Primate A member of the most highly developed order of animals, including apes, monkeys and human beings.

Radioactive Giving off powerful rays at a rate that becomes slower as time goes by. Measuring the rate of radioactivity tells us the age of some types of rock.

Reptiles Cold-blooded creatures with scaly skins whose young are produced in eggs.

Scavenger An animal that feeds on the remains, droppings, or leftover food of other animals.

Species A group of animals that can breed together to produce young like themselves, which are also able to breed.

Picture acknowledgments

The publishers would like to thank all those who provided photographs for this book: by courtesy of the British Museum (Natural History) 4; Survival Anglia Limited 9 (Alan Root), 11 (Mike Linley), 22 (Jeff Foott); ZEFA 18. The photograph on page 29 belongs to the Wayland Picture Library.

Further information

You can find out more about evolution by reading the following books:

Amazing Facts about Animals by Gyles Brandreth. Doubleday, 1981.

Dinosaurs and Other First Animals by Dean Morris. Raintree Publishers, 1977.

Dinosaurs and People: Fossils, Facts, and Fantasies by Laurence Pringle. Harcourt Brace Jovanovich, 1978.

Ecosystems and Foodchains by Francene Sabin. Troll Associates, 1985.

Evolution Goes on Every Day by Dorothy H. Patent. Holiday, 1977.

Fossils by Neil Curtis. Franklin Watts, 1984.

How Animals Behave by Donald J. Crump, ed. National Geographic Society, 1984.

How Animals Live by Philip Steele. Franklin Watts, 1985.

How Life on Earth Began by William Jaspersohn. Franklin Watts, 1985.

If You Are a Hunter of Fossils by Byrd Baylor. Scribner, 1980.

Life before Man: The Story of Fossils by Duncan Forbes. Dufour, 1967.

The Story of Evolution by L.B. Taylor. Franklin Watts, 1981.

It is worthwhile to visit a good natural history museum, where you can see displays on fossils and evolution. You may also wish to join an organization that helps to protect wild animals from extinction. Some useful addresses are:

Audubon Naturalist Society of the Central Atlantic States
8940 Jones Mill Road
Chevy Chase, Maryland 20815
301-652-9188

The Conservation Foundation
1717 Massachusetts Avenue, N.W.
Washington, D.C. 20036
202-797-4300

Greenpeace USA
1611 Connecticut Avenue, N.W.
Washington, D.C. 20009
202–462–1177

The Humane Society of the USA
2100 L Street, N.W.
Washington, D.C. 20037
202-452-1100

The International Fund for Animal Welfare
P.O. Box 193
Yarmouth Port, Massachusetts 02675
617-362-4944

National Wildlife Federation
1412 16th Street, N.W.
Washington, D.C. 20036
202-797-6800

Index